Research & Education

Regional Economic Development: Research & Education

Jess Browning

Bainbridge Island, WA 98110

Research & Education

Bronco ePublishing, LLC
Bainbridge Island, Washington

Regional Economic Development: Research And Education

ISBN-13: 978-1981748044
ISBN-10: 1981748040

First published 2017.

Some copyright material referenced is under terms of the GNU Free Documentation License http://en.wikipedia.org/wiki/GNU_Free_Documentation_License.

For Creative Commons Licenses see their websites http://creativecommons.org/licenses/by-sa/2.0/deed.en and http://creativecommons.org/licenses/by-sa/3.0/

Key Words: economic development, innovation, labor, theory, chaos, frame work

Regional Economic Development

Research & Education

BOOKS IN PRINT

Black & White Non-fiction

Technology, the Economy & Jobs: A Historical Perspective

Ancient European Ancestors (A Grey Tones Edition)

Brownings in England (A Grey Tones Edition)

Captain John Browning (A Grey Tones Edition)

Jess and his Family: Genealogy and History (Grey Tones Edition)

Global Logistics and Trade: Intermodal Transport

The Innovation Process: Educating and Teaching

Respect for Labor

The Deceitful and Insidious Web

Seattle to England by Surface Transport

The First Amendment: Speech Freedom

Color Non-fiction

Ancient European Ancestors: The DNA, Archeological, Historical and Linguistic Evidence

Browning's in England: Records of where, when & how they lived

Captain John Browning: A Family History in England & Virginia from 1255 to 1799 AD

Jess and his Family: Genealogy and History

Black & White Historical Fiction: Short Stories

The Nomads: Their Migration Experiences

The Anglos: Their Pleasures and Travails

Southwest England: Life and Times 1390 to 1430 AD

Research & Education

Captain John: From England to Virginia
Francis: Plantation Owner, Merchant & Tobacco Farmer
Caleb: The Frontier Man
Jeb: His Family and History
William T.: A Man to Look up to
China: 1979

Black & White Collected Short Stories

Anatolia to Britain: A Trilogy
America's Frontier: Virginia to California
Compendium of Short Stories: From Eurasia to Seattle

Black & White Biographies

Life and Times of Jess Sr.
Life and Times of Anna Love.
Jess Jr.: A DIY Guy
Cec and Caroline: A Wonderful Life!
Vicki: A Cheerleader
Some Swank Descendants
Some Perdue Descendants

Books Edited & Re-written

Four Centuries 1611-2017: The English Bible

King Arthur Series Volume One

King Arthur & Modred: A Young King in Waiting
King Arthur & Sir Balin: A Knight with Two Swords
King Arthur & Pellianore: A Father of Knights
King Arthur & Sir Gawain: Their Adventures
King Arthur & Rome: Ambassadors Demand Tribute

King Arthur & Lancelot: Their Fights & Affairs

King Arthur & **Gareth***: The Kitchen Boy*

King Arthur & Tristram: The Fighter

King Arthur & Knights: Lovers & Fighters

King Arthur Series Volume Two

King Arthur & Lancelot: Book X, Volume Two

King Arthur & Lancelot: Book XI, Volume Two

King Arthur & Lancelot: Book XII, Volume Two

King Arthur & Lancelot: Book XIII, Volume Two

King Arthur: Percivale: & Lancelot Books XIV-XV, Vol. Two

King Arthur & Gawain: Book XVI, Volume Two

King Arthur & Galahad: Book XVII, Volume Two

King Arthur & Queen's Joy: Book XVIII, Volume Two

King Arthur: Guinevere & Lancelot Book XIX, Volume Two

King Arthur & Gawain: Book XX, Volume Two

King Arthur & Mordred: Book XXI, Volume Two

Research & Education

CONTENTS

Research & Education

DEDICATION

This book is dedicated to all who have endured the time spent by the author on its research, writing, editing and publication.

It is especially dedicated to Morgan D. Thomas who was a great teacher and friend.

The book is also dedicated to the referenced sources noted which were of great help in providing a work that is hoped to be of educational value to the broader community. The inclusion of these sources adds immensely to the story presented in a critical manner and the brief nature of its inclusion has no reflection on its value.

Specific citations are given when information is available and when not available credit is given based on the source.

Research & Education

INTRODUCTION

Professor Morgan D. Thomas, was past President of both the Western Regional Science Association in 1961 and the Regional Science Association International in 1975. He was a leader in regional economic development research and education. He was well known for his research and teaching in the field of regional economics. His specialization dealt with the role of innovation and technology in regional economic growth theory. The author of this book referenced Professor Thomas' work in an earlier study, which concentrated on the role of technology, and economic theory in government policy to promote economic development and jobs. Excerpts of Thomas' contribution in the study are presented in this book as they were categorized earlier. The main categories include structural change, unemployment and government policy; conceptualizing structures and processes; theories and employment change; technological change and trajectories; and policy decisions.

A conceptual framework that is based on Professor's Thomas' teaching is presented. It was developed by the author to organize and explore linkages between theory and policy. The elements making up the framework include "technological change", "economic theories", "forces influencing change", and "policy decisions". The framework was used to show how structural change as related to technological change can be impacted by policy decisions that may, or may not, come from accurate interpretations of economic theories.

The author began studying under Professor Thomas in 1990 and was the Professor's last Ph.D. student. The author also worked under him first as a TA and later, in 1991 as an assistant, when Thomas was Associate Dean in the College of Arts and Sciences at the University of Washington in Seattle. Both Thomas and the author spent many hours together working and discussing regional economic development theory and policy. Professor Thomas was a good friend and mentor. The author wishes to acknowledge him for his support and inspiration.

Research & Education

CHAPTER ONE: Morgan D. Thomas

Professor Morgan Thomas was past President of both the Western Regional Science Association in 1961 and the Regional Science Association International in 1975 and was a leader in regional economic development research and education. He was well known for his research and teaching in the field of regional economics. His specialization dealt with the role of innovation and technology in regional economic growth theory.

Professor Thomas had many students and colleagues from the University of Washing that were involved in the RSA. Some of those included past presidents, for example: William L. Garrison (1962 RSA); Charles M. Tiebout (1965 WRSA); Edward L. Ullman (1970 WRSA and 1960 RSA); Richard L. Morrill (1993 WRSA); and Geoffrey J. D. Hewings (2001 RSAI and 2007 WRSA). Some of Professor Thomas' prominent Ph.D. graduates included William B. Beyers and James W. Harrington in addition to those listed as his Ph.D. students at the end of this book.

Professor Thomas retired at the end of 1996 and a large commemorative party was held for him on March 3, 1997 in Seattle. He served as Professor of Geography and Associate Dean of Arts and Sciences at the University of Washington for almost 40 years. He passed away August 6, 2001 and hundreds of former colleagues, friends, and students attended his memorial service.

The following book is based on some of Professor Thomas's work and is extracted from the author's study titled *Technology, the Economy, and Jobs: A Historical Perspective.*[1] It concentrates on the role of technology and economic theory in government policy in promoting economic development and jobs.

Regional Economic Development

Research & Education

CHAPTER TWO: Problem & Outline

This book is based on some of Professor Thomas's work and is extracted from the author's study titled *Technology, the Economy, and Jobs: A Historical Perspective.*[2] It concentrates on the role of technology and economic theory in government policy in promoting economic development and jobs.

Based on Professor's Thomas' teaching, a conceptual framework was developed by the author to organize and explore linkages between theory and policy (see Figure 5) in the United Kingdom over a sixty-year period from the 1930s to the 1990s. The elements making up the framework include "technological change", "economic theories", "forces influencing change", and "policy decisions". The policy making process for these regions was researched to see how the role of technology, in the process of economic change has been articulated.

In the study, economic theories were summarized and economists considered influential in the policy process were identified.

Associations were made between government policies created during the period of the study and the forces influencing those policies. An analysis of the work discussed evidence of implicit or explicit references to "technological change" or "technological possibilities" in policy discussions. It was found that technological advance, and investment in education, new products, processes, industries, and undertakings was explicit. What was lacking, however, was the idea of a "model" which could make the role of technology in economic development more explicit and meaningful.

Using the framework, an attempt was made to show how structural change as related to technological change can be impacted by policy decisions that may, or may not, come from accurate interpretations of economic theories.

The following sections reference Professor Thomas' work that was used in the author's study regarding technology and structural change. This first section discusses the impact of structural change on employment in regions and the response of economic theorists and government policy maker's to the adverse effects of that change. The spatial nature of structural problems is addressed by introducing geographical questions, which are then synthesized into variables from which hypotheses are drawn.

The Economic Geographer's Perspective:

Thomas states that a geographer may look for explanations of economic activities and their relationships to growth where the scale of growth is linked with the power and influence of various interests and institutions. In looking at economic growth, he may look at forces over long periods. He may have an appreciation for the sense of process. He may be concerned with studying the effects of new technology on growth and change of regions and within regions. He may want to know why some regions grow and some don't.[3]

Conceptualization by the geographer always involves the question of scale and scale depends on the positioning in space and time of one's mental perspective. If one is thinking about the behavior of firms in an industry, one is conceptualizing at a micro level. If one is thinking about trade between regions, one is conceptualizing at the macro level. To understand how spatial systems are created and change over time, there needs to be a theoretical framework that considers not only the spatial economic aspects of technology and industry but also the social needs and behavior of groups of individuals at certain times or over certain periods.

Regional Economic Development

Research & Education

CHAPTER THREE: Structures & Processes, Conceptualization

This section presents an overview of the global economy going back to 1930 and describes the turbulent era of the 1960s and 1970s when the process of industrial change began to significantly transform the world economy. It describes the emergence of transnational corporations, new industrial strategies and new government policies. It discusses structures and processes of growth and decline, then introduces the study regions and describes their socioeconomic conditions from the 1930s to the 1990s. The section elaborates on the continuing problem and process of structural change in industrially developed regions that may result in economic decline and social problems. An ontological structure was created in order to contextualize the cross disciplinary nature of the elements used in the conceptual framework. Both the structure and its conceptual elaboration for application to development were used to help organize and discuss what is known about economic theory, government policy, influential forces and the role of technology in economic change.

Structural Change, the Global Economy, Organizational Changes and Long Term Planning

Thomas states that the organizational structures developed during the Second World War by governments to promote efficiency and quality in industrial production provided models that were later adapted to assist firms, which were moving toward long term planning. In a number of industrialized countries, a national commitment to deal with perceived economic problems around the world came into being; and plans were developed to identify and correct economic problems through direct and indirect foreign investment. In conjunction with this determined attitude, there was also an emphasis on quantitative measures for measuring economic growth. The Keynesian principle that high unemployment could be traced to insufficient aggregate demand, and that the latter could be "manipulated" was in vogue, and expenditure policies were initiated to solve problems by providing problem areas with capital intensive investment in factories using low wage labor. These factories used efficient, mass-production technology and the cost per person was high.[4]

He states that in the decade of the 1950s, as countries were still rebuilding after World War II, growth in the US, Italy, Japan and West Germany, especially in manufacturing, was more rapid than in other countries. A new wave of multinational high technology firms spread overseas (especially from America), first with exports and then with direct investments. Markets in Canada and Europe attracted US investment, and the construction of new plants and acquisition of subsidiaries by US firms within these countries was a significant factor in economic growth.[5]

In the United Kingdom, it was a matter of bringing factories to the people. Other methods provided incentives for workers to migrate to more prosperous areas, and factories to move to less prosperous areas.

There were disincentives to building factories in prosperous areas. Subsidies to factories, firms, and people were also provided in some areas. Experiments with these types of solutions continued into the following decades.

The 1960s and 1970s: A Global Shift

Thomas states that economic growth reached unprecedented levels during the 1960 to 1970 period with international trade increasing more rapidly than production. There had been a fourfold increase in world trade between 1960 and 1968. Also during this period, fundamental processes related to structural change began to emerge. There was an increase in the internationalization of economic activities, an increase in commodity prices and an increase in labor costs. The composition of manufactured exports changed as the proportions of such basics as textile and clothing declined and metals remained static. The most rapid growth was in higher technology products such as machinery, transport equipment and chemicals.

Meanwhile, in addition to the oil shortage, globalization of industry, a relative decline in manufacturing jobs, and a relative increase in service employment, social change was taking place.[6]

In North America and Western Europe, there was a concern about the increasing scale of urbanization, congestion, pollution, and their impact on quality of life and growth. These changes were beginning to have an effect on world trade, industrial transformation, and development. These were inflationary times during a period of deep recession especially in long established heavy industries such as steel making. The combination of inflation and recession led to the term "Stagflation" coined by John H. Cumberland in the 1970s.

Thomas said that many people were unaware that a process of deep structural change was taking place. The leveling of economic growth did, however, give industry and academia time to reflect on the quality aspects of economic life and on the globalization of industry.[7] Figure 1 shows the traditional view of the macroeconomic structure.

As late as 1990 the majority of economists influencing labor (unemployment) and economic development policy were still advocating either public spending (expenditure) or monetary policy based on Keynesian and Neoclassical economic theories. These were theories that relied upon the premises of maximization of behavior at all levels and equilibrium of the economic system.

Regional Economic Development

Research & Education

CHAPTER FOUR: Stagflation: A Failure of Traditional Economic Theories

Thomas states that the traditional solutions of Keynesian and Neoclassical economic theories could not cope with "stagflation", this new condition of inflation without growth and high levels of unemployment. By the 1980s, the depressed economic conditions at national and sub-national levels became the concern of various governments and their academic advisors, especially where regions of high unemployment were an issue of concern.[8]

The problem of structural change was not being addressed in traditional theories and yet the statistical evidence of change had been clear for more than a decade; and even longer with respects to the shifts out of the primary sector and the rising productivity in terms of output per labor input in many sectors of the economy. In the US, the amount spent on research and development (R&D) in business began to decline in 1963-1964. To those following the teachings of economists Kuznets, Mensch, Kondratiev, and

Schumpeter at the time, these data would have indicated a decline in industrial expansion. Thomas states however, that very few of the traditional economists were thinking about Schumpeter and his ideas of "creative destruction" or of industrial change, especially deep structural change, until the later 1970s.

Aspects of Structural Change

Structural change reflects a change in the composition of sectors and industries within a given economy and may extend to other world economies. Structural change often results from the decline of a particular industrial sector within a region. Traditionally industrial structures do not remain viable in older industrial countries. Within regions, older traditional industries tend to stagnate or decline.

Thomas states that the future may be viewed gloomier than the present. Regions with older declining industries will generally have below standard social conditions or unhealthy social structure. They often have unsightly urban areas, a lack of supporting services and their public and social infrastructure is generally neglected and deteriorating. The infrastructure revolves around the older and declining industries. The occupational structure of the region tells about the nature of the work, skills, and level of education. This is important, since workers in declining industries tend to lack the skills for new higher technology however; public sympathy is likely to be evoked for "old job protection." As industries decline, the workforce earns less money and GNP growth is slowed.[9]

He states that at the end of the 1960s, there was a decline in productivity both in the US and Europe as workers income went up, but their real income lagged. Individual consumption functions were changed and more family members needed to work to maintain family consumption levels. The number of people in manufacturing declined, yet in the early 1970s there was no universal explanation for why this happened.[10]

Descriptions of structural change include various dimensions such as prices, technology, social attitude, political processes, institutional forces, market forces, inertial forces, consumption, migration, and specialization. Figure 2 shows a breakdown of resource relationships.

Regional Economic Development

Research & Education

CHAPTER FIVE: Conceptualizing Economic Development

Structural Change and Economic Policy

In reviewing literature from the 1930s to the 1990s, it was found that the context, in which policy was written and implemented, needed to be examined in order to see how a policy or a sequence of policies affected economic development. It is a process that was found to be very difficult to track, but the philosophical and theoretical context behind policies is important. Policy makers who want to research and to develop appropriate policy instruments to deal with socioeconomic problems resulting from structural change should be interested in the ontology of philosophies that are behind economic theories in order to be as objective as possible in their evaluation of alternatives. Economic development consists of long-term processes, which contain extremely complex phenomena.

Economic theorists have been unable to provide a comprehensive explanation of these phenomena, and other conditions, under which economic activities grow and decline within a region. Their explanations are made more difficult by a lack of information needed to evaluate the spatial, technical, economic, organizational, and other characteristics that influence the economic activity in a region.

Traditional theoretical approaches have tended to be at the macro scale and also tend to be based on statistical relationships between the economic development in a region and the aggregated variables of labor, technology, education, taxes and capital. These theories have tended to ignore the spatial relationships of the region's industries, firms, and establishments and the influences on these tendencies created by the region itself over time.

Thomas states that the factors of production include the region's population and its workforce; its occupational structure, industries; firms and establishments; its social and economic infrastructures; its sets of laws and government policies as well as incentives and regulations; its institutional structures related to education and social and commercial activities; its minerals, timber, water, climate and other natural resources or elements; and its location relative to other regions and places. Over time, the region may attract new economic activity, which makes it difficult for factors to equalize.[11] Figure 3 shows the resource relationships.

CHAPTER SIX: Theories & Employment Change

This section looks at economic theorists' conceptualization of the structural change that took place in several regions of the U.K. since 1930. The study examines these theories and subsequent policies based upon them, with attention to earlier schools of thought to provide the necessary grounding for exploring later works. The study moves forward from 1950 to the late 1970s where a threshold was crossed in economic growth and development theory with the introduction of "technological paradigm" or "set of technological possibilities". This is related to Kuhn's scientific model, which he describes as, a ". . . universally recognized scientific achievements that for a time provide model problems and solutions to a community of practitioners."[12] Goodall describes a paradigm as ". . . a 'supermodel' which provides intuitive and inductive rules about the kinds of phenomena scientists . . ." within a discipline ". . . should investigate and the best method of investigation."[13]

Thomas states that Classical and Neoclassical economics deals with both macro and micro levels of economic activity, but this type of activity reveals only the aggregation or disaggregation of activity for a particular economic system and usually a closed system at that. Economic geography has dealt with location decisions by firms and industries for resources, production, and markets; but, for the most part, has also relied upon equilibrium and the rational behavior of Neoclassical economics. Thomas states, in his early research, that Neoclassical economic theories could not provide answers to the dynamics of regions and industries in Northern Ireland, and that that he had to go back to records of manufacturing in the 18th century to get a degree of understanding about the process. In looking at the long run, he realized that economies were influenced by factors developing over many years, not months, and that there are changes in a population's tastes and preferences plus changes in technology.[14]

Theories of Economic Growth: Standards and Performance

Short-term and Long-term Economic Growth Theories

Money and Economic Growth

Thomas states that equilibrium in theory pertaining to money and economic growth "required desired savings to equal desired investment." Friedman's monetary theory states that, once workers have come to expect a given rate of price inflation, any attempts by government to reduce the level of unemployment by expansionary fiscal policies creates pressures to raise money wages, thus neutralizing the reduction in unemployment while generating more inflation.[15]

CHAPTER SEVEN: Growth Theories
Neoclassical Growth Model

In Solow's theory, Thomas states that growth is achieved by new strategic assumptions. His assumptions are, "at each instance in time, all labor and capital is thrown on the market" and "Quasi rents and wage rates will adjust immediately to clear the market." Thomas states that Input prices will adjust to assure the desired capital/output ratio. The system could then always adjust to a given labor supply ". . . in such a manner that the full employment of labor and the satisfying of entrepreneurs are achieved at the same time, not accidentally but by a substitution of inputs responding to changed factor prices." Thomas says that this theory, and its models, treated the economy as one large firm producing for one large consumer, but this type approach concealed variables that may or may not contribute to economic change.[16]

Conditions Underlying Long-term Economic Growth

Denison, Kaldor, Kuznets, Lewis, Nelson, and Thomas all write about conditions for long-term economic growth. Using the Cobb-Douglas model. Thomas states that there are five conditions, which will enhance the probability that growth will take place:

1) Following a rise in productivity (usually from technology) which may result in an autonomous rise in the income of a population which will increase demand for a higher output; there follows an increase in effective demand, which in turn - through the accelerator and income multiplier - induces further rise in real income per-capita. Effective demand is real because of purchasing power and a demand for commodities from the existence of rise in real income. A real and induced rise relates to the income multiplier and export base.

2) *A growth in output capacity tends to accompany such changes and expansion of capacity would also tend to follow an increase in effective demand for the regions which creates a larger market for a regions products external to the region (income multiplier and export base).*

3) *When the rate of increase in the value of region's net injections or exports is greater than the rate of increase of net leakages or imports.*

4) *When there is an improvement in the regions trade - national as opposed to sub-national; and*

5) *When there is a postponement in consumption in the region.*[17]

CHAPTER EIGHT: Spatiotemporal Theories of Economic Growth

Economic Base/Export Base

Thomas states that the Export Base theory uses similar analysis to that of strategic factors in the development stages theory. The dominant factor is the export sector and the growth of net exports. A competitive edge is established along with a cost advantage over other regions due to a combination of specialization (cheaper), better products, and transport cost advantages. The Basic activity or export base component is a relationship between the export sector composed of the export shipper and external import industries. The Non-Basic component is the Residentiary Sector. This sector is dependent on the employees of the Basic Sector. The level of activity in the basic sector is set by forces outside of the area, and changes in this sector will result in changes in the non-basic sector that will result in increases or decreases in the total employment and population. Basic sector activities are the mechanism for transmitting effects of external income shifts to the home area. Increase (decreases) in demand for products of the basic sector will result in the increase (decrease) of total activity within the area. The magnitude of these changes is determined by a basic/non-basic ratio. For the continuing growth of the economy, this model needs net exports to generate income for investment. The model does not consider technological advance or the disposal of net income.[18]

Growth poles and growth centers

A valuable economic theory regarding growth centers and "growth poles is discussed by Perroux, Hirshman, Boudeville, Hansen, Pred, Higgens, and Thomas. Thomas states that Perroux began dealing with the dynamism of growth poles at the macro and national level by looking at propulsive industries which induced growth in other industries through linkages. His theories provided a mechanism for showing growth in a short period because the forces could die quickly. Others began to question how to identify forces that will insure growth will continue over a long period of time.[19]

Thomas identified a strategic factor, the Engel effect, which ties together the importance of the role of income elasticity of demand with capital and technical change to explain the role of a "propulsive industry" in growth pole theory. This Engel effect, in which a reduced demand in proportion to income may result in a surplus of purchasing power which may lead to new products and industries to absorb this surplus in income. This concept became another proximate cause of economic growth. When a propulsive unit begins to move and draws inputs, it induces growth. A lot depends on income increases and income elasticities. If coefficients remain constant, the production functions are unchanged and then one changes technology, there will be a change. If one changes products, the system will change.[20]

Thomas states that Perroux alludes to long periods where things must change. The income multiplier and accelerator will take care of the indirect effect of the propulsive industry and induced growth from linkages. The income multiplier and accelerator impacts take time. When induced effects take place, hypothetically, one reaches equilibrium. The input industries meet the needs of the propulsive industry and all levels out. Therefore, a new growth effect takes place or several growth poles in one country. When the source of the impulsive thrust of the poles or firms reaches equilibrium, a new source is needed. [21]

Thomas also refers to Kaldor who states that in order to achieve self-sustained growth or long-term economic growth, two conditions must be present. The first is that the demand for commodities must be present and the second is that returns must increase. Thomas then states that self-sustained intensive economic growth also requires the satisfying of the condition of increasing returns. This is possible when one is able: (a) to bring about a more rapid accumulation and application of per capita knowledge, capital, and other resources in production; and (b) to reduce the costs and increase the efficiency of the uses of inputs so as to reduce the unit costs and increase the supplies of output.

He says that if the condition of increasing returns is met, one may assume that within a region a rise in productivity is experienced resulting in an autonomous rise in real income. There follows an increase in effective demand which in turn - through the accelerator and income multiplier - induces further rise in real income. A growth in output capacity tends to accompany such changes and expansion of capacity would also tend to follow an increase in effective demand for the region's product in external markets. When a firm's average unit costs are lower through efficiencies brought on by technological innovation, it lowers its price for outputs to customers. Thus, it may sell more which affects input from its suppliers. More input from the suppliers creates multiplier effects and internal economies expand at a rapid rate. There is positive output in the economy and strong linkages are developed with others in the region. The firm's prices are down, incomes are up and purchasing power is increasing. The Engel effect comes into play resulting in more demand for goods and services and, in turn, income multiplier linkages come into play. A greater demand for consumer goods results in more demand for capital stock which is known as the accelerator effect. The use of an input-output framework and forward-backward linkages are an important methodological aid in developing this concept.[22]

Flexible Production and Division of Labor (post-Fordism)

Thomas says that the disaggregation of industries by theorists that began to take place in the mid 1950s has progressed down to the reorganization of firms at the plant level (opening the black box) which has greatly increased the explanatory task.[23]

Reorganization of firms at the plant level has resulted in a shift from vertical integration where the goods that used to be moved by forklift on the factory floor to horizontal integration where outsourcing put the same goods on trucks, trains, boats, and planes.

Thomas states that technological innovation became the "new causality" for explaining economic growth and changes in the composition of sectors, and was incorporated as mechanical, macro-economic relationships into Neoclassical growth theory. This modified theory did not, however, allow for explaining the process of innovation over time or space and led to a re-examination of the "stages of growth" models which further led to "stages of development" models.[24]

Stages of Growth, and Stages of Development

Over time, it became apparent to some economists that most economies go through stages of growth and development. This theory is expounded upon by Clark, Rostow, and Thomas. Rostow's "Stages of Growth" model states *"the economic history of any economy may be differentiated into five stages:*

(1) traditional — limited technology, subsistence agriculture and poorly developed commercial economies;

(2) preconditions for takeoff — external and internal stimulus by investment in infrastructure and agricultural equipment; new social and political units led by an enterprising elite evolves;

(3) takeoff — to sustained growth over 20-30 years; continued investment, manufacturing becomes stronger, resources are exploited and a political, social and an institutional framework that encourages growth emerges;

(4) drive to maturity — application of modern technology to all phases of economic activity; diversification carries the economy beyond the initial industrial activity, first triggering

growth, then the economy becomes self-sufficient; and

(5) mass consumption — consumer goods and services begin to rival heavy industry and the population develops consumption levels beyond its basic needs.

Thomas states that Rostow's theory is extended into the development stage theory. He states that theorists zeroed in on this determinism in the 1960s and that some characteristic of this concept still have merit. One component is a broad aggregated analysis of three sectors that have always followed a determinate pattern in industries of industrialized countries. In the First stage, a consumer goods industry dominates. In the Second stage, the capital goods industries are increasing with a net of about one half that of the consumer goods industries. In addition, in the Third stage, there is a balance of the consumer goods industries and capital goods industries. However, toward the end, the capital goods industries will expand more rapidly. This may lead to a fourth stage in which capital goods may be more important. According to Thomas, the key to the ". . . development stage theory mainly rests on the society's ability through technological innovation and greater divisions of labor to produce the same output with a smaller input of resources thereby releasing a supply of resources for an expansion of existing industries and the creation of new industries." Thomas states that the Stages of Development theory suggests a sequential path of development through which all nations' progress, reflecting changes in the dominant occupations of the labor force following changing comparative costs and autonomous change in income elasticity of demand (tastes and preferences change). The Engel demand elasticity consumption function does not increase as fast as income which leads to a surplus of new products and commodities in economic activity; and that this consumption function, leading to reduced demand for staples in proportion to income, may lead to new industries to absorb the surplus in income.

Thus, income elasticity leads to mechanisms for structural change based on the Engel curve.[25]

International: Long-Waves and Cycles

Long wave theory came into discussions of economic growth at the national level but the theory has not been rigorously studied in a sub-national or context. In the 1970s and early 1980s, many economists began to look for a more disaggregated approach to the study of innovation and technological change. High technology firms and industries began to offer promise to those areas experiencing decline and economic stagnation; and policy makers began to concentrate on innovation promotion, and technology oriented policy instruments.

Thomas states that certain economists and geographers began to come together on economic and spatial research questions regarding innovation and technical change, and while there has been a converging of effort by economists and geographers on the role of innovation and technological change, there continued to be a need for a better conceptual framework.[26]

Over the last two decades, life-cycle frameworks have been created by theorists dealing with the dynamics of socioeconomic change at national and sub-national levels.

Innovation Cycles

The innovation cycle as discussed by Thomas is closely related to "long wave" theory in explaining how economies recover from a slump. The innovative cycle or time path has two stages: (1) invention is followed by innovation which is the first commercial application of the new product; and (2) subsequent product innovations modify the product and process innovations improve production efficiency. Not all firms in a new product industry will necessarily carry out innovative activities throughout the innovation cycle of the new product. The innovator firm for the new product need not be, and usually isn't, the first innovator for all subsequent product and/or process innovations. Thomas states that the process of innovation includes an entrepreneurial function which consists of unlearned acts of insight - the entrepreneur. This function can only be carried out by the entrepreneur or by an entrepreneurial group, There is also a managerial function which consists of learned acts of skill. This function can be carried out by both the entrepreneur and managers.[27]

CHAPTER NINE: Human Behavior: Individuals and Entrepreneurs

Thomas states that over the last 50 years, there has been an attempt to humanize studies in economic and social systems. Every so often, a society rebels against the mechanical interpretations of life or why people think or philosophize in a certain way. They say, "let's humanize things." This is an age-old concern. Thinking about societies in the abstract all the time loses touch with reality. There is a need to get down to the micro foundations - to see the workers going in and out of the factories and to watch the pieces of product going by. There is a need to humanize it and to think of what the human beings are thinking or experiencing rather than their robotic capability. Human behavior may be simulated in a production setting but a robot cannot be made to feel like a human being. It is important to distinguish between people and robots. When thinking about the behavior of mechanical things, the conceptions concerning such phenomena are fairly finite. When thinking about the behavior of human beings which may be affected by feelings, the conceptions concerning this type of phenomena will have many more possibilities. Mechanical behavior will be different than human behavior.[28]

Research & Education

CHAPTER TEN: Evolutionary Economics

Thomas states that most development economists were schooled in the idea of maximizing behavior, but some began to question the utility of these ideas and whether there was a proper understanding of the causal factors in economic systems. Not all accepted the idea of equilibrium and they began to explore the uncertainties and to question what causes an individual or a firm to maximize profit and utility? They began to disaggregate the economy using input-output models to look at accumulations of information about individual sectors which could perhaps be used to quantify uncertainty. They began to look at the qualitative measures of change with the idea that inputs and outputs may reflect both quantitative and qualitative measures. Some theorists had been looking at input - output analysis, the export base theory, development stages theory, and growth poles in the search for explanatory factors of economic growth and technological change.[29]

Schumpeter and the Entrepreneur

Joseph Schumpeter is famous for his term "creative destruction" in going head to head with a competitor in business. Thomas was a great student of his and Schumpeter's work is of particular interest. Thomas states that an important contribution by Schumpeter is the distinction between price theory and behavioral concepts. Innovations are a vital source of competition and may lead to what he termed "creative destruction.

> *"It is not . . . price . . . but competition from the new commodity, the new technology, . . . the new type of organization . . . competition which commands a decisive cost or quality advantage and which strikes not at the margin of the profits and the outputs of the existing firm but at their foundations (firms in competition) and their very lives."*[30]

Innovations in new products, processes, and in management may provide a competitive advantage and when done successfully firms will grow. Schumpeter's theory is bound to the successful firm. However, success may be effected by other dimensions besides that of the entrepreneur's efforts. It may be affected by time and place; by temporal and spatial dimensions; by being in the right place at the right time. The act of carrying out entrepreneurship is enterprise. The entrepreneur is distinct from the managerial function, but the managerial function may be carried out by the entrepreneur. The entrepreneurial function only shows up in innovation. It is not easy to identify.

Early work by Schumpeter was on industries made up of small firms. His later works bring in the larger and multinational firms where innovation is carried out in R&D and executives make the decisions. His focus is on the behavior that depends on intuition - a grasping of the essential facts. The success of an entrepreneur is based on the unlearned innate acts of insight. The non-routine versus routine acts of managers. Normally the manager's behavior is learned rather than intuitive. Frequently innovative behavior is accompanied by high levels of skill. Schumpeter's innovation is a new production function. This is a discontinuity for the neo-classical economist who looks for a new combinations of factors and who is interested in the changing production functions of the leading firms and economies.

Thomas states that Nelson and Winter, in their "Evolutionary Theory of Economic Change" do not use production function - it is too restrictive. To them, the intangible is the important factor rather than a new combination of factors in production.[31]

Research & Education

CHAPTER ELEVEN: Technological Change & Trajectories

In this section, the study identifies new technology as an impelling force in economic growth and describes how this plays a role in economic development at national and sub-national levels. It sets the stage for exploring the role of governments, industries, and institutions in creating policy for regions in industrial decline. It contextualizes structural change within in a "technological model" and further describes Kuhn's "scientific Model". In looking at the role of technology in this context, the study also provides a background for the policy-making process in Britain at different socioeconomic levels over a period of 60 years.

Income elasticity of demand is a strategic variable and over time, excluding the effect of transfer payments, intra-and intergrowth impulses are transmitted through the dynamic technological, income multiplier, and accelerator linkages. Technological change carries a dual role as it influences the possibilities of achieving cost efficiencies and productivity increases which represent contributions to the achievement of conditions of increasing returns and the growth of new industries through the creation of new products. Thomas states that these are the conditions which provide the basis for a conceptual framework to explore the relationships between technological change and intensive growth.[32]

Regional Economic Development

CHAPTER TWELVE: Technological Change and Industrial Structures
Long-Wave Theory and the Entrepreneur

Thomas states that according to Schumpeter, innovations are introduced discontinuously, and in swarms, because of the way entrepreneurs appear. They are the innovators - not the inventors but the pioneer leaders in business - who are endowed with the qualities required to depart from the current routine and break new paths. They function in swarms because daring calls forth more daring and an innovation in any field tends to spread through imitation and to give rise to further innovations, first in the same field and then elsewhere in fields that are technically or economically related. In short, Schumpeter states that the entrepreneur and innovations are responsible for the process and dynamism of long-run economic development. Schumpeter states that the entrepreneur and the process of innovation is a metaphysical relationship with innate "unlearned acts of insight."[33]

As noted earlier, Thomas says there is a managerial function and an entrepreneurial function. The former can pertain to both entrepreneurs and managers, but the entrepreneurial function pertains only to entrepreneurs. It is a part time function which is a function of leadership as owner, manager, leading person, etc.[34] The entrepreneur can change the production function of his or her firm as innovation combines factors in a new way and requires carrying out new combinations.

Thomas says that innovation is also a vital source of "behavioral competition" or "creative destruction".[35] He says that in Schumpeter's later model, the entrepreneurial function may consist of a group or a team in the innovative process. The "learned acts of skill" are becoming increasingly important in the study of non-routine decision making associated with the process of innovation.[36] These are the types of individuals and organizations who effect change and from all of this, one may infer that firms which innovate successfully will grow.[37]

Research & Education

CHAPTER THIRTEEN: Policy Decisions

This section looks at the policy makers' responses to structural change in several regions of industrialized Europe since 1930. At the supra-national government level, the study looks at policy decisions in the European Union and how the EU has brought these policies to bear on various levels of groupings of member states and industrial concerns within the EU. In Britain, it looks at how government departments and ministers responsible for policymaking and policy implementation have transformed economic ideas into initiatives.

Policy Making and Government

The *ends*, the results of political choice, and the *means*, the policy, should be examined by developing a set of political choices. Policy needs to be dealt with in a political manner. Disparities represent a political force strong in the core and weaker in the perimeter.

Thomas states that one needs to think of theorists in sets of classes. This person is coming from a certain perspective. It's all political. It may need agreement on criteria. He states that one needs to be looking for conceptualizations that are better than those we have. Classical location theory does not allow time to bring in radical change in technology or whatever may come along. Small changes lead to large accumulated changes. One needs to theorize at the micro level looking at private firms in a capitalist society. The problems reflect an interest in dealing with policy implications that are governed by those who are interested - the politician. The purpose is important. There are a set of problems and all should be taken into consideration. There needs to be a consideration of the background and a need to focus on variations in a particular country - this requires a classification scheme. There needs to be a focus on the problem as related to industries keeping in mind important kinds of industrial structure and socioeconomic conditions.[38]

Undeveloped regions, for example, do not usually have the same kinds of resources that the developed or underdeveloped regions do. Thus greater policy intervention would probably be required if a government deems it necessary to improve the income (or subsistence) level of an underdeveloped region's population. Thomas states that macro thinking has dominated policy thinking but it hasn't done much good. It was not identifying the forces bringing about change and affecting competition. Therefore, there was a need to explore processes at the micro level in order to build a better macro economy.

In developing various criteria to solve problems there is a chance for great disagreement. For example, the Labor party in UK and the Democrats in the US tend to advocate the public approach for solving problems whereas the Conservatives in the UK and the Republicans in the US are looking for a private way through the market to solve the problems. Thus, different viewpoints provide a lot of room for debate. It is a clash of an equity approach and an efficiency approach. Thomas states there has been too much focus on the region and not enough on the people. Policy needs to include both and needs to be more explicit about the human element.[39]

Policy Generation

Thomas states that technology is a factor of emerging significance in economic theory and economic development policy. It is a factor that needs to be incorporated into good theories for explaining socioeconomic problems as well as into good (appropriate) policy instruments to deal with these problems. A desire to raise per capita income is a reason for policy. In addition, unemployment which is a social problem as well as an economic problem is a good reason for policy. Economic theory needs to deal with the real problems that exist in the world. Going back in time, one needs to think of the context in which economic theory was written and how it was used to develop economic policy that would require implementation. One needs to think that it was "this event, this sequencing of events affected these forces, etc."[40] It is something that is very complex and, very difficult to track.

In order to better understand what was happening in a regional economy, a framework for conceptualizing processes was developed as shown in Figure 4. Based on this a conceptual framework was derived that can be used to illustrate the influnceing forces and resultant policy actions (see Figure 5).

CHAPTER FOURTEEN: CONCLUSION

Thomas states that in Schumpeter's work of 1907-1909, published in German in 1911, the individual entrepreneur was much more important in firms of that time than they are in contemporary firms. In his final book, the 1950 version, "Capitalist Society and Democracy," he described the crucial role of the entrepreneur and the part his innovations must play to insure economic growth in a capitalist system. Schumpeter had stated this earlier in his "Theory of Economic Development" which came out in 1934.[41]

Thomas states that in order to deal with economic development theory, one needs to fully understand the nature and significance of the entrepreneur and the innovation process. It requires the study of these phenomena as integral elements of a dynamic social economic political system. Schumpeter was very much aware of this, but he took the stance that many other social scientists have taken by claiming "I don't know how to deal with some of these other unknown dimensions; I am a trained economist." He dealt with social and political forces in his work, but had to put in a disclaimer. He was only concerned with the economic factors that would be endogenous in whatever model of the economy he was dealing with.[42]

Thomas states that in this type of approach, the development of a dynamic economic, social and political theory, requires a multidimensional model. Critical social theorists today believe they have one, but they are unwilling to accept the capitalist system. And that is the system that most scientists actually must deal with in today's developed world. Schumpeter noted, "the use of the second best approach involves an abstraction forced upon us by the tactical conditions of mentally copying reality."[43]

The conceptual framework for economic development presented enables one to better understand the factors of production and the processes that promote or impede technological development and resultant economic development. Figure 6 shows the impact of the various schools of thought on the six levels of resouces in a regional economy.

FIGURES

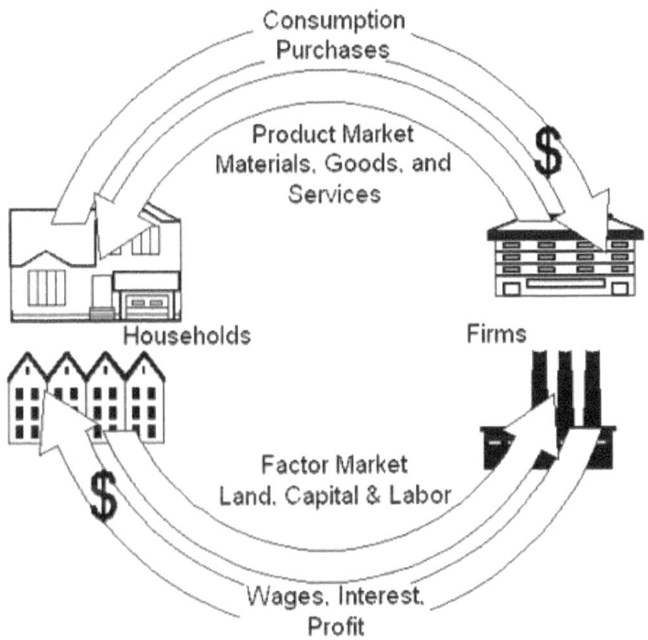

FIGURE 1: Traditional Macroeconomic Structure

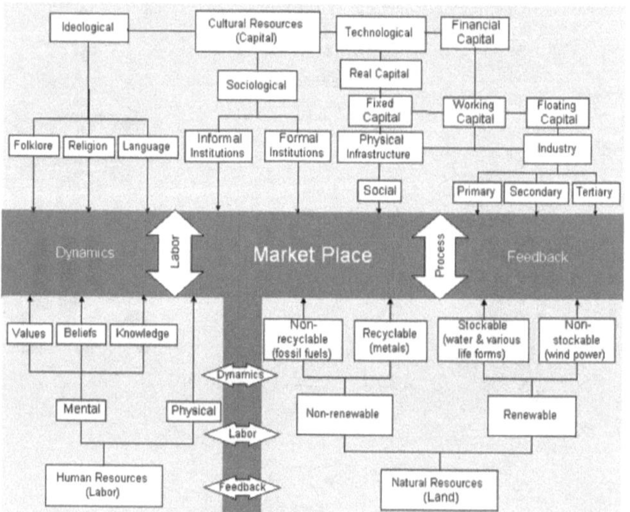

FIGURE 2: Earth's Resources - Labor, Land, and Capital

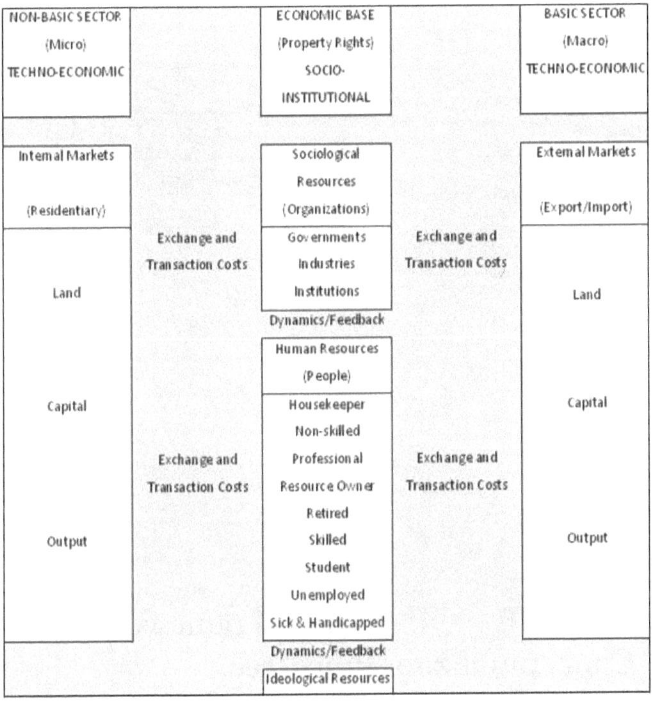

FIGURE 3: Resource Relationships

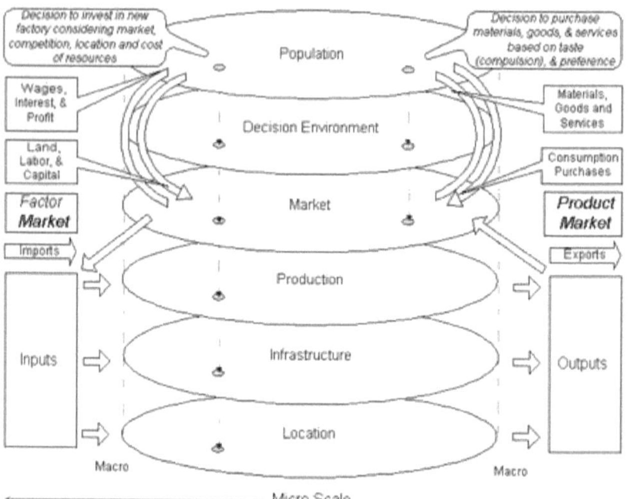

FIGURE 4: A Framework for Conceptualizing Processes

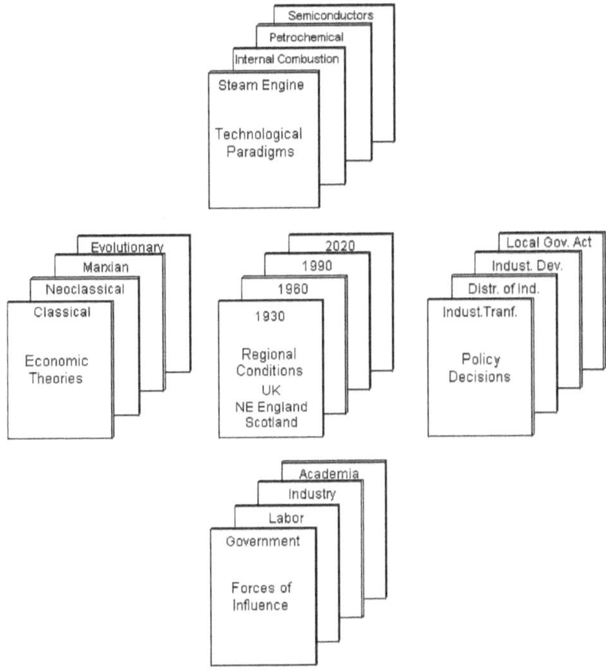

Elements Influencing and Effecting Change within a Region

FIGURE 5: Conceptual Framework - Economic Development

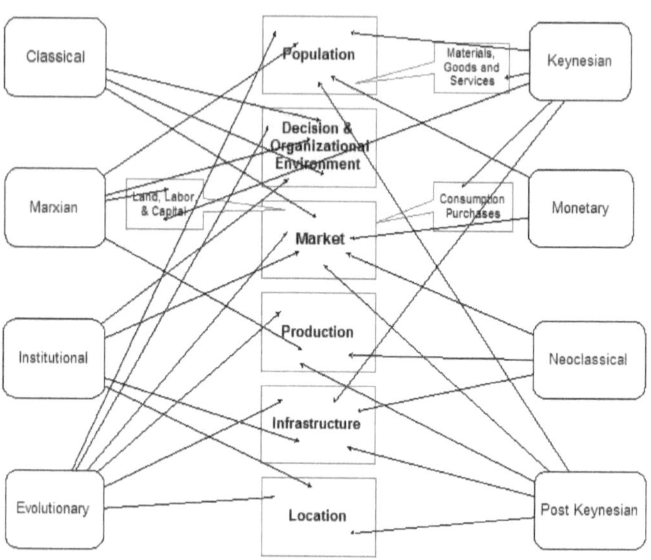

FIGURE 6: Economic Schools of Thought and Structures

GRADUATE (Ph.D.) STUDENTS

Deane Richard Lycan. *Defense-Space Research and Development Contraction Expenditures: Analysis and Some Implications of Their Areal Patterns.* [1964]

Anne Buttimer. *Some Contemporary Interpretations and Historical Precedents of Social Geography: With Particular Emphasis on the French Contributions to the Field.* [1964], IGU President, 2001.

Douglas Knowles Fleming. *Coastal Steel Production in the European Coal and Steel Community 1953 to 1963.* [1965] [University of Washington]

Guy Perry Frederick Steed. *A Framework for the Study of Manufacturing Geography: With a Consideration of the Nature and Process of Manufacturing Changes in Northern Ireland 1950 to 1964.* [1966]

Günter Krumme. *Theoretical and Empirical Analyses of Patterns of Industrial Change and Entrepreneurial Adjustments: The Munich Region.* [1966] [University of Washington]

John Brian Parr. *Regional Development and Public Policy: North-West England and the Post War Period.* [1967] [University of Glasgow]

William Bjorn Beyers. *Technological Change and the Recent Growth of American Aluminum Reduction Industry.* [1967] [University of Washington]

David Williams Wilcoxson, Jr. *The Economic Geography of the Contemporary Steel Industry in the American West.* [1967]

Neil Robert Michael Seifried. *A Study of Changes in Manufacturing in Mid-Western Ontario 1951-1964.* [1969] [University of Alberta]

John Campbell. *The Relevance of Input-Output Analysis and Digraphg Concepts to Growth Pole Theory.* [1969]

James B. Cannon. *An Analysis of Manufacturing as an Instrument of Public Policy In Regional Economic Development: Canadian Area Development Agency Program 1963-1968.* [1969]

Charles W. Moore. *Growth poles and industrial linkage development paths; a research methodology.* [Urban Planning, 1971] [Natural Resources Canada]

Rodney A. Erickson. *The "Lead Firm"; Concept and Economic Growth: An Analysis of Boeing Expansion, 1963-1968.* [1973]

Peter Harrison. *The Land Water Interface in an Urban Region: A Spatial and Temporal Analysis of the Nature of Significances of Conflicts Between Coastal Uses.* [1973]

Richard Le Heron. *Productivity Change and Regional Economic Development: The Role of Best-Practice Firms in the Pacific Northwest Plywood and Veneer Industry, 1960-1972.* [1973] [Auckland]

Charles Gilbert Smith. *Spatial Structure of Industrial Linkages and Regional Economic Growth: An Analysis of Linkage Changes Among Pacific Northwest Steel Firms, 1963-1970.* [1973]

Kwawu Yao Agbemenu. *The Pattern of Growth in the Manufacturing Industry in Ghana, 1958-1969.* [1974]

James William Harrington. *Locational Change in the US Semiconductor Industry.* [1983]

Barbara Lynn Brugman. *A Spatial Perspective on the Process of Technological Innovation in Technology-Intensive Industry.* [1983]

Godfrey Emmanuel Chisanga. *The Wood Products Industry of the Lower Columbia Region: Technological Change, Evolution and Its Role in Regional Economic Development.* [1983]

Patrick Aldwell. *Technological Rejuvenation and Competitiveness in the Washington State Woodpulp Industry, 1960-1985: A Global Perspective.* [1988] [Lincoln University, Canterbury, NZ, 2001]

Edward Joseph Delaney. *New Firms' Innovative Search In A New-Technology Industry: Evaluation of Biotechnology Firms.* [1991]

Jesse Harrison Browning. *Regional Development, Technological Paradigms and Policies: A Framework for Conceptualizing Socioeconomic Processes.* [1995] [GTTL, University of Washington, Seattle]

Regional Economic Development

BIBLIOGRAPHY

Thomas, Morgan D., Thomas, M.D. *Growth and Structural Change: the role of technical innovation*. In Amin, Ash and John Goddard. <u>Technological Change, Industrial Restructuring, and Development</u>. London: Allen & Unwin, 1986.

Thomas, Morgan D. *Growth Pole Theory, Technological Change, and Economic Growth*. In the <u>Papers of the Science Association</u>, Vol. 34, 1975.

Thomas, Morgan D. *Economic Development and the Role of Innovation and Technical Change*. Chapter 2 in <u>The Economic Impact of Technological Change</u>. Eds A.T. Thwaites, R.P. Oakey, London: Frances Pinter, 1985, p.p. 18-21

Thomas, Morgan D. <u>*Schumpeterian Perspectives on Entrepreneurship in Economic Development: A Commentary*</u>. London: Pergamon Journals Ltd., <u>Geoforum</u>, vol 18. no. 2, 1987.

Thomas, Morgan D. *The Export Base and Development Stages Theories of Economic Growth: An Appraisal*. In <u>Land Economics</u>, 40:421-432; No. 4, Nov., 1964.

PAPERS & PUBLICATIONS

Thomas, Morgan D., Conceptualizing the Role of Innovation in Industrial Change and Development, 1988

Thomas, Morgan D., Innovation and Technology Strategy: Competitive New Technology Firms and Industries. In: Giaoutizi, M., P.Nijkamp and D.Storey, eds., Small and Medium Size Enterprises and Regional Development. London: Croom Helm, 1987.

Thomas, Morgan D., The Innovation Factor in the Process of Microeconomic Industrial Change: Conceptual Explrations. in: E. Wever and G.A.van der Knaap, eds., New Technology and Regional Development. Beckenham: Croom Helm, 1987.

Thomas, Morgan D., Schumpeterian Perspectives on Entrepreneurship in Economic Development: A Commentary. Geoforum 18(2), 1987, 173-86.

Thomas, Morgan D., Growth and Structural Change: The Role of Technical Innovation, in: A Amin and J. Goddard, eds., Technological Change, Industrial Restructuring and Regional Development. London: Allen & Unwin, 1985.

Thomas, Morgan D., Regional Economic Development and the Role of Innovation and Technological Change in: Thwaites,-A.-T., ed.; Oakey,-R.-P., ed. The Regional Economic Impact of Technological Change. New York: St. Martin's Press (or London: Pinter), 1985, 13-35.

Thomas, Morgan D., Structural Change and Selected Dimensions of Technological Change, in: Geographia Polonica 45, 1983, 83-95.

Thomas, Morgan D., Industry Perspectives on Growth and Change in the Manufacturing Sector, in: Rees, Hewings, Stafford (1981), pp.41-58.

Thomas, Morgan D., Growth and Change and the Innovative Firm, Geoforum 12(1), 1981.

Thomas, Morgan D., Explanatory Frameworks for Growth and Change in Multiregional Firms Economic Geography 56(1), Jan. 1980, 1-17.

Thomas, Morgan D., Economic Development, Technological Change, and the New International Economic Order, Geoforum 10(2), 1979, 129-40.

Thomas, Morgan D., Some Explanatory Concepts in Regional Science, Presidential

Address, Regional Science Association, Toronto 1976, in: Papers, Regional Science Association 39, 1977, 7-23.

Thomas, Morgan D., Perspectives on Technological Change and the Process of Diffusion in the Manufacturing Sector, (with Le-Heron, Richard B.) Economic-Geography; 51(3), July 1975, pages 231-51.

Thomas, Morgan D., Economic Development and Selected Organizational and Spatial Perspectives of Technological Change Economie-Appliquee; 28(2-3), 1975, 379-400.

Thomas, Morgan D., Growth Pole Theory, Technological Change and and Regional Economic Growth, Papers, Regional Science Association, vol.34, 1975, 3-25.

Thomas, Morgan D., Structural Change and Regional Industrial Development, in: Spatial Aspects of the Development Process, Helleiner and Stoehr, eds., Toronto: Allister (for IGU Congress), 1974, pp.40-1.

Thomas, Morgan D., The Regional Problem, Structural Change and Growth Pole Theory, in: Growth Poles and Growth Centers in Regional Planning. A.R.

Kuklinski, ed., The Hague: Mouton, 1972, 69-102.

Thomas, Morgan D., Growth Pole Theory: An Examination of Some of Its Basic Concepts, in: Niles M. Hansen, ed., Growth Centers in Regional Economic Development. New York: Free Press, 1972, pp.50-81.

Thomas, Morgan D., Regional Economic Growth: Some Conceptual Aspects Land-Economics; 45(1), Feb. 1969, pages 43-51.

Thomas, Morgan D., Sequential Changes in Economic Activity Patterns: Some Comments, Annals (AAG), 54(3), 1964, 438-9.

Thomas, Morgan D., Resources and Regional Development: Some Comments, Papers, Regional Science Association, 13, 1964, 201-5.

Thomas, Morgan D., The Export Base and Development Stages Theories of Regional Economic Growth: An Appraisal. Land Economics 40 (1964), 421-32.

Thomas, Morgan D., Regional Economic Growth and Industrial Development, Papers, Regional Science Association 10 1963, 61-75. [1962 Zuerich Conference]

Thomas, Morgan D., Some Comments on the Development and Contemporary Uses of the Regional Method in the United States, Przeglad Geograficzny 33(2), 1961. (in Polish)

Thomas, Morgan D., Imports, Industrialization, and the Economic Growth of Lesser Developed Countries, Professional Geographer 13(5), 1961, 13-16.

Thomas, Morgan D., Programming, Industrial Interdependence and Economic Development, University of Washington Business Review, October 1960, 48-57.

Thomas, Morgan D., Economic Activites in Small Areas, Land Economics 36(2), 1960, 164-71.

Thomas, Morgan D., Estimates of Water Uses in the Muskingum Watershed Conservancy District for 1975, Annals (Association of American Geographers), 50(1), March 1060, 22-41.

Thomas, Morgan D., A Regional Model for Projecting Industrial Water Consumption, Papers, Michigan Academy of Science, Arts and Letters, XLIII (1958), 251-8.

Thomas, Morgan D., The Economic Base and a Region's Economy, Journal of the

American Institute of Planners. 23(2), 1957, 86-92.

Thomas, Morgan D., Manufacturing Industry in Belfast, Northern Island, Annals (Association of American Geographers), 46 (June 1956), 175-96.

Thomas, Morgan D., Economic Geography and the Manufacturing Industry of Northern Ireland, Economic Geography, 32(1), 1956, 75-86.

ABOUT THE AUTHOR

Jess Browning is former Director of Global Trade, Transportation and Logistics Studies at the University of Washington in Seattle. He has and MPA Degree from the University of Southern California and a Ph.D. from the University of Washington in Seattle.

At the local level he served on the Freight Mobility Roundtable; at the national level he served on the Transportation Research Board's International Trade and Transportation Committee; and at the International  level he served as a U.S. Delegate to APEC's Transportation Working Group.

In retirement, he helped form a Consortium of eight international universities to do joint research an education in the fields of business, advanced technologies, logistics and marine affairs.

Jess is a former entrepreneur having engaged in manufacturing and global trade. He holds eight patents in environmental and process control equipment.

He believes that economic development takes place at many scales that includes: *from what takes place on the plant floor to what takes place in various regions of the world.* He finds no difficulty in moving from one to the other in order to promote economic development.

Jess is and author of thirty four books and has edited five more with more to follow. He has given many talks, lectures and keynote addresses at home and abroad. He is married and lives with his wife near Seattle. They have 4 daughters, 6 grandsons, 4 granddaughters and 6 great granddaughters with 2 great grandsons and another known to be on the way.

INDEX

REFERENCES

---

[1] Browning, Jess, *Technology, the Economy, and Jobs: A Historical Perspective,* Bronco ePublishing: Bainbridge Island, WA, ISBN 978-1-4675-2263-2, 2012.

[2] Browning, Jess, *Technology, the Economy, and Jobs: A Historical Perspective,* Bronco ePublishing: Bainbridge Island, WA, ISBN 978-1-4675-2263-2, 2012.

[3] . Thomas, M.D. Lecture, Geography 500, Autumn 1990.

[4] . Thomas, M.D. *Growth and Structural Change: the role of technical innovation*. In Amin, Ash and John Goddard. Technological Change, Industrial Restructuring, and Development. London: Allen & Unwin, 1986.

[5] . Ibid., Thomas (1986).

[6] . Ibid.

[7] . Ibid

[8] . Ibid

[9] . Thomas, M.D. *Growth and Structural Change: the role of technical innovation*. In Amin, Ash and John Goddard. Technological Change, Industrial Restructuring, and Development. London: Allen & Unwin, 1986. & G466

[10] . Ibid., Thomas (1986) & G466

[11] . Thomas, Morgan D. *Economic Development and the Role of Innovation and Technical Change*. Chapter 2 in The Economic Impact of Technological Change. Eds A.T. Thwaites, R.P. Oakey, London: Frances Pinter, 1985, p.p. 18-21

[12] . Kuhn, Thomas S. The Structure of Scientific Revolutions, Second Edition, Chicago: The University of Chicago Press, p. viii, 1970.

[13] . Goodall, Brian. The Penguin Dictionary of Human Geography". New York: Viking Penguin, Inc., 1987.

[14] . Thomas, Morgan Geography 500 Lecture Autumn 1990. Thomas was schooled in Neoclassical models of

economic growth and studied for his Ph.D. on manufacturing in the early 1950s in Belfast, Northern Ireland.

[15]. Thomas, M.D. *Growth and Structural Change: the role of technical innovation*. In Amin, Ash and John Goddard. Technological Change, Industrial Restructuring, and Development. London: Allen & Unwin, 1986.

[16]. Ibid

[17]. Thomas, Morgan D. *The Export Base and Development Stages Theories of Economic Growth: An Appraisal*. In Land Economics, 40:421-432; No. 4, Nov., 1964.

[18]. Ibid.

[19]. Thomas, Morgan D. *Growth Pole Theory, Technological Change, and Economic Growth*. In the Papers of the Science Association, Vol. 34, 1975.

[20]. Thomas, Morgan D. *Economic Development and the Role of Innovation and Technical Change*. Chapter 2 in The Economic Impact of Technological Change. Eds A.T. Thwaites, R.P. Oakey (Frances Pinter, London) 13-35, 1985, p.p. 21-24; See Arthur Lewis (Chapter 4 in section on "Conditions Underlying Long-term Economic Growth").

[21]. Thomas, Morgan D. *Growth Pole Theory, Technological Change, and Economic Growth*. In the Papers of the Science Association, Vol. 34, 1975.

[22]. Ibid., Thomas (1975.)

[23]. Thomas, Morgan D. *Economic Development and the Role of Innovation and Technical Change*. Chapter 2 in The Economic Impact of Technological Change. Eds A.T. Thwaites, R.P. Oakey (Frances Pinter, London) 13-35, 1985.

[24]. Ibid, p.p. 18-21

[25]. Thomas, Morgan D. *Growth Pole Theory, Technological Change, and Economic Growth*. In the Papers of the Science Association, Vol. 34, 1975.

26. Thomas, Morgan D. *Economic Development and the Role of Innovation and Technical Change*. Chapter 2 in <u>The Economic Impact of Technological Change</u>. Eds A.T. Thwaites, R.P. Oakey (Frances Pinter, London) 13-35, 1985, p.p. 18-21

27. Thomas, Morgan D. *Economic Development and the Role of Innovation and Technical Change*. Chapter 2 in <u>The Economic Impact of Technological Change</u>. Eds A.T. Thwaites, R.P. Oakey (Frances Pinter, London) 13-35, 1985.

28. Thomas, M.D. Geography 466 lecture, Winter 1990.

29. Thomas, Morgan D. *Economic Development and the Role of Innovation and Technical Change*. Chapter 2 in <u>The Economic Impact of Technological Change</u>. Eds A.T. Thwaites, R.P. Oakey (Frances Pinter, London), 1985, p. 14.

30. Thomas, Morgan D. Schumpeterian Perspectives on Entrepreneurship in Economic Development: A Commentary. London: Pergamon Journals Ltd., Geoforum, vol 18. no. 2, 1987.

31. Ibid; Thomas, Morgan D. *Economic Development and the Role of Innovation and Technical Change*. Chapter 2 in <u>The Economic Impact of Technological Change</u>. Eds A.T. Thwaites, R.P. Oakey (Frances Pinter, London), 1985, pp. 13-35.

32. Thomas, Morgan D. *Growth Pole Theory, Economic Change and Economic Growth*. Papers of the <u>Science Association</u>, 34 3-25, 1975.

33. Thomas, Morgan D. *Schumpeterian Perspectives on Entrepreneurship in Economic Development: A Commentary.* London: Pergamon Journals Ltd., <u>Geoforum</u>, vol 18. no. 2, 1987.

34. Ibid., Thomas (1987), pp. 173-4.

35. Ibid., Thomas (1987), p.174.

36. Ibid., Thomas (1987), p. 185.

37. Ibid., Thomas (1987), p.174.

[38]. Thomas, Morgan D. *Economic Development and the Role of Innovation and Technical Change*. Chapter 2 in <u>The Economic Impact of Technological Change</u>. Eds A.T. Thwaites, R.P. Oakey, London: Frances Pinter, 1985 and Geography 466, Winter 1990.

[39]. ibid., Thomas (1985 and 1990).

[40]. Thomas, Morgan D. Geography 466 Lecture, Winter 1990.

[41]. Thomas, Morgan D. <u>*Schumpeter*</u>*ian Perspectives on Entrepreneurship in Economic Development: A Commentary*. London: Pergamon Journals Ltd., <u>Geoforum</u>, vol 18. no. 2, 1987.

[42]. Ibid., Thomas (1987).

[43]. Thomas, M.D. Geography 466 lecture, Winter 1990.